Healing Numbers of
Solfeggio Frequencies

ISBN 978-981-18-2622-1

LifeQuest Training Hub Pte Ltd
https://elearning.LifeQuest.sg/LifeSound
Email: info@lifequest.sg

Acknowledgments

This book is nothing short of my labor of love. It took a lot of effort from my end. Involved in already a number of commitments, I found it hard to devote my full energy and effort to this book, but I knew I had to do it. Just like solfeggio frequencies changed my life for the better, I wanted the same to happen to everyone else, at least those who read this book, if not more.

This beautiful book, yes beautiful because I can hear the rhythm and harmony of solfeggio frequencies beating in it, could not have been possible without the constant love and support of some truly important people in my life.

I am indebted to my wife Zoe Ee and my daughter Ching Yee for their love and trust in my capabilities and for being in my corner always.

My adept and amazing co-workers and assistants Sandy Chang and Penny Chong made sure I stick to this book, and to give it a shape. Their efforts are genuinely appreciated and acknowledged.

I am also grateful to all the volunteers who took part in carrying out the research for this book. They listened to the frequencies, and made sure to oblige to my instructions for four whole months, which is nothing sure of great. Thank you Chang Ek Fong, Chloe Pei, Christyn Teo, Dolise Siow, Joanne Chan, Lau Meo Leng, Lilys Tan, Patrice Leong, Skylark Teoh and Wenny Chin.

All of you have played a huge role in bringing this book together, and I'll always be thankful to all of you.

Lastly, I'd like to thank all my readers for taking out the time to read this book. I promise you it will bring undeniable transformation and happiness in your life.

Author Bio

Master Thomas Chiam is a passionate educator with over 12 years of experience as a numerologist. Throughout the years, Thomas has distinguished himself as a knowledgeable, visionary leader with an outstanding ability to create revolutionary instructional methods that impact people's lives and enhance holistic learning. Thomas holds the Association Internationale de Numerologues Asia (AINA) certifications of numerology with Certified Practitioner Members (CPM) and Certified Higher-Level Consultants, NumerLife Certified Consultant Members (NCCM).

Thomas views education as a powerful tool that can effectively empower and transform people's lives with better knowledge and awareness. With this view, Thomas had an aim to create an educational system that took a holistic approach to learn, built on a model that brought out the best in learners through numerology. This vision came to life in the form of LifeQuest Academy, which he founded in 2009.

Thomas's natural love for numbers has led him on a path of continuous learning and sparked in him a relentless desire to build his knowledge and share it with others. His passion for numerology and metaphysics and excellence in developing inventive ideas in these fields have deservedly earned him respect among his peers.

Further, Thomas's works reflect his great focus on detail and an intricate thought process – aspects that have preceded his reputation and recognition as a respectable authority on the world's numerology stage. Over the years, Thomas has taught and trained thousands of students on numerology from different parts of the world. He is renowned for using simple, fun, and interactive techniques to explain complex concepts. He continually encourages his students to explore diverse approaches to a problem, thus helping them develop critical thinking skills.

Thomas is the Founding Chairman of the Asian International Numerology Association (AINA), a Council Member of the International De Numerology Association, UK (AIN), and the creator of LifeCards, an oracle deck founded on ancient symbols and numbers. One of Thomas's most remarkable works is the "Healing Numbers of Solfeggio Frequencies," his brainchild's concept that empowers people to draw on their birth dates to master and leverage the power of solfeggio frequencies. He seeks to unravel the relationship between solfeggio frequencies and the ancient Chinese Lushu in I-Ching and explore numerology and its link to the frequency of solfeggio tunes. Even if this is your first time coming across solfeggio frequencies, you will be amazed by their unimaginable powers as you read this book.

Introduction

All of us go through some kind of pain in life. Challenges in different forms surround us.

Sometimes they come in the form of a financial crisis. Sometimes as relationship problems. Sometimes as the loss of a loved one. Sometimes in the form of feeling disconnected from your spirituality and lacking a sense of purpose in life. The bottom line is we do go through different kinds of struggles, and every battle brings forth a different sort of pain and disturbance in life.

While we do move on with life and try to power through, sometimes, it so happens that we feel stuck in a rut. No matter how hard we try, we find it difficult to move ahead, treat our painful experiences as bygones, and combat challenges with resilience. It just doesn't seem doable.

This inability to move on is rooted in many issues, including chronic stress and grief, fear, insecurities, self-doubt, negative thoughts, toxins in the body, chemical imbalances, lack of spirituality, limiting beliefs, and even genetic issues.

All these issues keep us from advancing in life, living in

the moment, exploring and honing our potentials, creating balance and harmony in life, and feeling empowered from within.

But what if I told you there exists a perfect solution to all these problems?

What if I told you that you could heal all your self-doubts, negativities, and insecurities and become a reservoir of love and happiness?

What if I told you that you can attain good health, wealth, love, abundance, success, and everything you have ever wanted?

And what if I told you that the simple antidote to all your problems and to have everything you desire for lies in music?

You must have heard of the old age adage 'music is food for your soul,' but did you ever contemplate the science behind it?

Did it ever occur to you to check up on the phrase and see if there is any reality to it?

The truth is, this phrase is accurate because all the issues I mentioned above and all the positive improvements that you seek in your life can be easily achieved with the help of music. In this case, **'solfeggio frequencies.'**

Sounds quite interesting, right? It is actually as soothing and as intriguing as it seems to you too.

If you are alien to this term, you should know that solfeggio frequencies are specific tones of sound that help heal various issues regarding your mental, emotional, spiritual, and physical health. When the concerned problems are cured, you feel healthy, active, energetic, and positive, and find it easy to function optimally.

These frequencies date back to the ancient eras and are believed to be the elemental sounds frequently used in Eastern Indian and Western Christianity religions, chanted by priests, monks, gurus, saints, and literally everyone who wished to promote better healing in the body and mind.

English poet, playwright, and actor, Shakespeare once said,

'If music is the food of love, play on.'

Many of us don't know that music is actually the food of health, healing, love, happiness, abundance, and a lot more. It is a source of inspiration to many and is often likened to being a universal language. Like every other language, music too has gone through an evolution with time.

That said, most of us limit music to only rock and roll, blues, classical, gospel, indie pop, jazz, or other such genres. We either forget or are unaware that music has a vibrant history believed to be rooted in spirituality.

You will come across a lot of literature crafted on music and its therapeutic effects on mood. Music is about energy, frequency, and vibration. You may not know this, but human beings and every living being and inanimate object in this universe are composed of energy that vibrates at specific frequencies.

When specific frequencies complement each other, they are drawn towards each other. This is governed by the phenomenon of *'like attracts like,'* which proves how we attract positive experiences by nurturing positive thoughts.

Also, specific energy vibrations are so powerful that they promote healing in your body. This is precisely what Solfeggio frequencies do. Solfeggio frequencies are associated with energy, mathematics, spirituality, light, and inner healing. They slowly fix all the abnormalities in your body, mind, and spirit to cure the many ailments you experience, so you start to thrive in the world. Many of us are new to the power of numerology. Every number has a certain vibration that has different effects on us. In this manner, numbers of the solfeggio frequency do have certain powers associated with them that, when harnessed, can improve your life for the better.

It is understandable to be intrigued by Solfeggio frequencies and be interested in exploring this music further to move closer to your best life to date. Precisely this is why I have crafted this book for you- to help you explore and embrace the world of Solfeggio frequencies so you too can reclaim your life.

This book is a detailed blueprint on Solfeggio frequencies. It talks about the origin of these frequencies, the science behind them, how they promote healing in the human body, mind, and soul, and why you must incorporate them into your life. Moving on, I will also educate you on how to:

- Reap the benefits of these frequencies by experimenting with the nine solfeggio frequencies to release guilt and fear
- Decrypting the 9 solfeggio frequencies with numbers to heal yourself
- Trigger transformation in your body and mind to

create miracles for yourself

- Promote happiness and love in your life
- Detox your body and improve your self-expression
- Awaken your intuition
- Experience relief from stress and pain
- Rejuvenate your body and activate your pineal gland
- And so much more!

I assure you that you will be in awe of the amazing wonders in the universe, and you'll fall more in love with the solfeggio experiences with every page that you read of this book. By the time you wrap up this book, you will already have started using solfeggio frequencies in your daily routine and will be motivated to stick to them for good.

Ever since I became exposed to the world of solfeggio frequencies, I have been hooked to them, and there has been no going back for me. I foresee the same happening with you, and I am super-excited to help you become a more empowered, confident, loving, and thriving being.

I worked on this book during the Covid-19 pandemic that has proven to be quite an unprecedented traumatic episode for all of us across the globe. Not only did it wreak havoc on our physical health and took the lives of many people around the world, it also subjected us to mental health challenges. When I discovered the extraordinary healing powers of the solfeggio frequency, I realized how the discovery happened at just the right time because right now is the time when people need such power the most.

Without further ado, let us start this journey to the phenomenal world of solfeggio frequencies. Let the healing begin!

TABLE OF CONTENTS

Chapter 1: Solfeggio Frequencies- What, Why, and From Where

Remember that 'Doe, a deer' song we sang in kindergarten, and maybe even after that?

Let us recall that together, and while we do that, I request you actually to sing it and then pay attention to how you feel soon after.

Doe, a deer, a female deer
Ray, a drop of golden sun
Me, a name I call myself
Far, a long, long way to run
Sew, a needle pulling thread
La, a note to follow Sew
Tea, a drink with jam and bread
That will bring us back to do (oh-oh-oh)

Maybe not too much, but I am sure you did feel a tad bit happy and light singing the song. Perhaps it brought back flashbacks of your childhood, those carefree days, the time spent in school with friends, and singing songs during music lessons.

This song lies at the foundation of solfeggio frequencies. The vocal note scale used in the song: do, re, mi, fa, so, la, ti, do is referred to as 'solfege' adapted from the invention of Guido D'Arezzo, a monk back from the eleventh century. Let us dig deeper into the origins of solfeggio frequencies and understand them better in this chapter.

The Origins of Solfeggio Frequencies

So Guido D'Arezzo invented some music that led to the creation of solfege: the vocal note scale mentioned above. D'Arezzo later experimented with different types of scales and curated many improvements in the music theory. His musical innovations have been used by many vocalists and music enthusiasts across the world.

In its most authentic form, solfege is found in the 'Hymn to St. John, the Baptist.' In it, the solfege starts with 'ut' and goes on to re, mi, fa, so, la.' This is exactly from where the story on solfeggio frequencies resonates.

Guido added a melody to the Hymn to St. John, the Baptist to help his music students understand how to sight-read any musical piece easily. During the eleventh century, Guido was searching for easier ways to teach harmonies and melodies to his monastic choirs. One of the techniques he used as a mnemonic tool known was the 'Guidonian Hand.'

Here, musical notes were linked with different places on the palm and fingers. When it was mastered, the choirmaster would point to the hand to guide the singers about the following note. This was a seemingly innovative way to learn music. Guido kept working on the method to improve it further.

Guido came up with the staff notations to teach hymns and chants to express an enjoyable musical scale easily. The original notations were 'UT, RE, MI, FA, SOL, and LA.' These are derived from the very first syllable of every half-line of the hymn mentioned above, which descends from the ancient work done by the eighth-century Roman poet Horace.

The scale of the six notes: C, D, E, F, G, A, the forefathers of the 'so, ra, I, fa, so, la, ti, do' later evolved into an advanced diatonic scale when 'UT' was changed to 'DO' sometime during the nineteenth century, and 'ti' was also added to it later on.

Before the advent of this melody system, different musical chants were passed down generation after generation of monks through rote learning, making them take around a decade to learn all about music. Guido revolutionized this approach, and his melody system made things a lot more convenient for everyone.

The system of musical notation and sight singing that we use today is the same as the one invented by Guido, with slight changes made to it. The solfeggio frequencies were extracted from this hymn, and the first stanza of it reads as follows:

Ut queant laxis
resonare fibris
Mira gestorum
famuli tuorum,
Solve polluti
labii reatum,
Sancte Iohannes.

'So that your servants may, with loosened voices, resound the wonders of your deeds, clean the guilt from our stained lips, O Saint John.'

The hymn is usually sung corresponding to a Gregorian chant, which is basically genuine do-re-mi music. This six-tone scale is believed to be readily used in the Gregorian chant afterward.

If wondering what the Gregorian chant is, it is a type of solo, sacred rather holy song with roots deeply embedded in the Roman Catholic Church. It underwent development in western and central Europe in the ninth and tenth centuries, with redactions and additions being made to it later.

Old Gregorian Book

Renowned German-American musicologist and author o many books on music, Professor Willi Apel, believes that the most peculiar thing about the 'Hymn to St. John, the Baptist' is that its first six lines start on the initial six notes of the scale, respectively. Every line's first syllable is then sung a note, just a degree higher than the initial syllable of its preceding line.

The interesting thing is that this is just the first half of the story. Let us move on to the second half now.

The Discovery of Solfeggio Frequencies

Carrying on with Apel's discovery, Dr. Joseph Puleo, a herbalist and neuropathic physician by profession, started researching the world of solfeggio frequencies sometime during the mid-1970s.

While thoroughly studying the Bible, he discovered that in verses 12 to 83 in the seventh chapter, six codes were repeated around the holy numbers 3, 6, and 9, and a series of these numbers.

He decided to decode these numbers and their series using the old Pythagorean approach of reducing verse numbers down to their single digit integers, which is now referred to as *'modular 9 arithmetic.'* He discovered that the codes showed a unique series of six extraordinary electromagnetic sound frequencies. What was more astounding about the discovery was that the sound frequencies paralleled to the six syllables extracted from the Hymn to St. John the Baptist as mentioned below:

UT, RE, MI, FA, SO, LA

even more impressive is that each of these corresponds to a color and hertz frequency with its qualities.

According to Puleo, these frequencies have certain characteristics and promote different functions in your body, mind, and soul. He deciphered these frequencies as mentioned below:

UT: This operates at a frequency of 396 Hz and is believed to liberate you of fear, insecurities, and guilt.

RE: This note functions at a frequency of 417 Hz and is in charge of undoing troublesome situations and facilitating change in your being and life.

MI: It has a frequency of 528 Hz and is believed to promote transformation in the body, mind, and soul and unlock miracles in life by repairing your DNA. It is extracted from the 'MI-ra gestorum phrase, which translates to 'miracle' in Latin. Experts claim that this is precisely the frequency genetic biochemists used to fix broken DNA which is the genetic blueprint responsible for creating life.

FA: Operating at a frequency of 639 Hz, this note is believed to govern creating connections and relationships in your life, as well as rehabilitating the strained relationships.

SOL: This particular note vibrates at a 741 Hz frequency and is known to awaken your intuition so you better tune into your gut feeling, recognize it and start making good use of it in your life to make better decisions.

LA: This note vibrates at a frequency of 852 Hz and helps you connect to your spirituality and unlock its

These are the six fundamental solfegg
Later. Dr. Horowitz worked on them and ap
patterns to discover these fundamental freque: .. uig up
three more.

174 Hz: This frequency is believed to be your body's natural anesthetic as it relieves all sorts of pain from the body and mind. It provides you with a higher sense of comfort and security and stimulates your internal organs to improve their overall functioning.

285 Hz: This is the frequency of regeneration of the body to attain a sense of optimism and wellness. It rejuvenates the energy levels of your body and mind at all levels and boosts your overall health.

963 Hz: This is referred to as the frequency of experiencing divine consciousness, so you attain a complete sense of oneness with the universe and its higher, spiritual power. It links us with the universe's power, so you can tap into it and unite yourself with it.

It is essential to wrap your head around the fact that every type of matter is constantly vibrating at a specific frequency. When something vibrates, it creates a sort of music, a rhythm, which means everything from a non-living item to a living being has its own specific melody.

Modern science has finally started exploring what ancient mystics discovered centuries ago: everything is constantly vibrating, from the tiniest dust particle to massive galaxies we cannot even imagine.

The rudimentary state of vibration is produced by sound. A frequency accompanies everything in the universe- its optimum vibration range, and this rate is referred to as resonance.

Now that you have clarity on the advent of the solfeggio frequencies let us further explore the science behind them, especially the association between solfeggio frequencies and numerology in the following chapter.

"The highest goal of music is to connect one's soul to their Divine Nature, not entertainment." - Pythagoras

Chapter 2: Solfeggio Frequencies, Numerology, and Cymatics

It is understandable how tricky it can be to decipher the true nature of the solfeggio frequencies, especially in numerology. It is, therefore, essential to explore this association better to understand the true power of the solfeggio frequencies.

Cymatics and Numerology

Cymatics refers to the science of understanding how sound and frequency affect matter, primarily in powder or liquid form. Swiss scientist Hans Jenny coined this term. He utilized a piece of special equipment that enabled one to see different shapes formed in a medium after being influenced by sound waves and frequencies.

Cymatic representation of each original solfeggio frequency

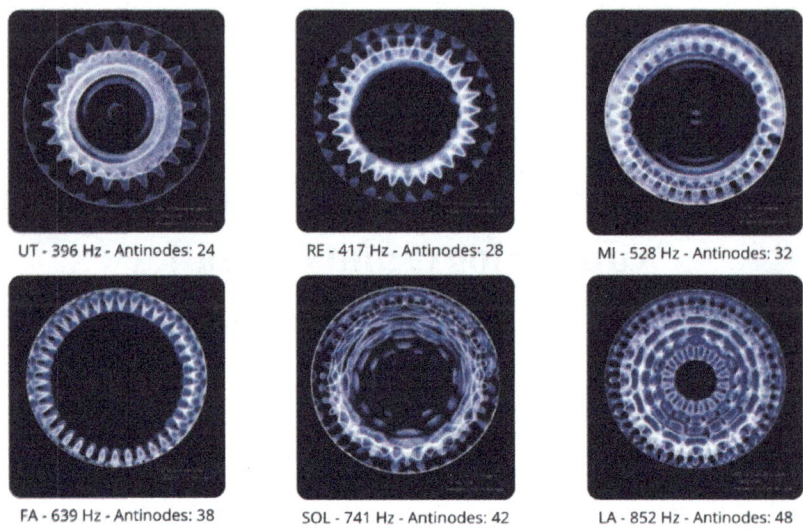

UT - 396 Hz - Antinodes: 24   RE - 417 Hz - Antinodes: 28   MI - 528 Hz - Antinodes: 32

FA - 639 Hz - Antinodes: 38   SOL - 741 Hz - Antinodes: 42   LA - 852 Hz - Antinodes: 48

Image courtesy of somaenergetics.com

SomaEnergetics, a company specializing in equipment and education for sound therapy, used a cymascope study to analyze and record cymatic images of the solfeggio frequencies. It was discovered that every image of the frequencies encompassed different nodes, aka the tops, and antinodes, aka the bottoms corresponding to the standing sound waves.

The researchers then counted the antinodes and discovered that majority of the solfeggio frequencies that could be created using tuning forks are easily divisible by the numbers 3, 6, and even 9. Any whole number divisor of the number 72 has a mathematical association between phi and specific frequencies: 2, 3, 6, 8, 9, and 12.

The numbers 3, 6, 9, and 12, particularly the first 3, have great power. All the numbers of the frequencies corresponding to the solfeggio frequencies can be reduced to these four numbers. When the numbers in the frequency 369 are added, the answer becomes 18, and when 1 and 8 are added, the answer is 9. When the numbers in the frequency 417 are added, the answer is 12, and when 1 and 2 are added, you get 3. Try breaking down all the numbers in the solfeggio frequencies, and the answer is likely to come out to 3, 6, and 9.

Nikola Tesla, the brilliant scientist and father of electro-magnetic engineering, with US and Serbian origins, once said,

'If you only knew the magnificence of the 3, 6, and 9, then you would have the key to the universe.'

This brings us to numerology, which is the divine science that states that every number has a deeper relationship with many coinciding events. The numbers: 3, 6, and 9 lies at the elemental root of the powerful solfeggio frequencies.

Numbers are the Language of the Universe

The base numbers starting from 0 going all the way to 9 hold great importance in the universe. A circle has 360 degrees, and if you add the individual digits in 360, you get 9, which is the same answer you get when you add the degrees in half a circle i.e. 180 degrees. This is also the answer you get when you add the individual digits in a quarter circle's degrees, i.e., 90 degrees. The total number of months in a year is 12, and when you individually add up the digits in 12, you get 3. Each day has 24 hours in total, and adding up the digits 2 and 4 gives you the answer' 6.'

These examples illustrate how mathematics is associated

with the entire universe. In fact, you can explain everything in the universe with the help of numbers, including the sun's position from Earth, the movements of all the planets, and how the different stars are distributed in the universe.

Numbers do not just encompass the physical aspects of our universe but extend to a large parameter and even cover the unseen universal forces, including the law of attraction and gravity law. Hence, understanding numbers and their power allows you to tap into the mighty force of the universe and deciphers the many miracles locked in it.

One of the most extraordinary phenomena in mathematics is the 'Golden Ratio.' Let us delve deeper into it.

The Golden Ratio

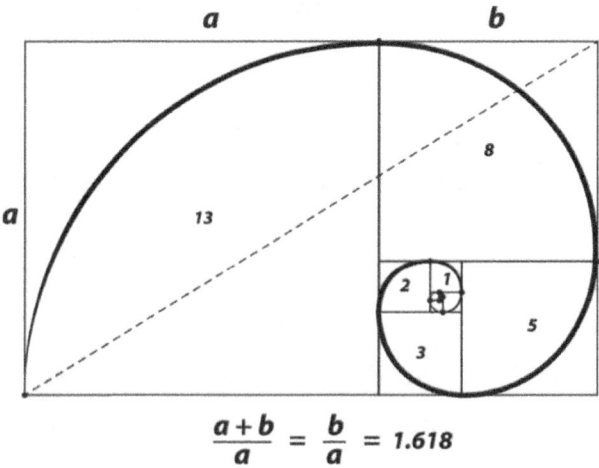

$$\frac{a+b}{a} = \frac{b}{a} = 1.618$$

This is an exciting mathematical ratio often represented by many natural objects all around us. It is a number that you get by dividing a line in a manner that the larger part's ratio divided by the line's shorter section comes out to be equal to the entire line's ratio divided by the larger part's length. The ratio you get as a result is not finite but forms an infinite number, so it is rounded off in the same way as the Pi (22/7) of a circle to 3.142.

The number representing this golden ratio is rounded off to 1.618. It is referred to as the 'Phi.' The golden ratio is also known by other names such as *the golden mean, the divine proportion,* and *the divine ratio.* Many ancient artistic and architectural works have exploited the divine ratio to produce brilliant results and striking designs.

The divine proportion is also exhibited in several natural phenomena and objects. Almost all the flowers have petals depicting the golden ratio. Secondly, this golden mean is also displayed in the shells, tree branches, and seed heads. Telescopic evidence has also shown that the universe observes a spiral pattern that once again follows the rhythm of the divine ratio. This proves the fact that this ratio has many mysterious applications in the entire universe. While all of its secrets are yet to be explored, many secret societies worldwide utilize a number of its mysteries to control different situations and events in our world.

Vortex

Vortex is used to describe a mass of fast rotating fluid with a tendency to attract different objects towards its center. Rotating ocean waves and whirlwinds are examples of vortexes. As per Mark Rodin's research, a vortex has great untapped power stored, which is also the divine power controlling all the universe's creations. It has some bases especially considering how our universe has a spiral shape, and the mighty power of wind and storms also follows the patterns of a vortex.

In Vortex mathematics, the sum of all the energies is 3, 6, and 9. Certain societies exploit the power tapped in the digits 3, 6, and 9 to rule the world. Mathematically, the universe is described by studying the shape of the geometrical circle with numbers 1 to 9 rendered on it. Lines are drawn to connect the numbers that depend on the resulting sum of the digits derived after the numbers are doubled.

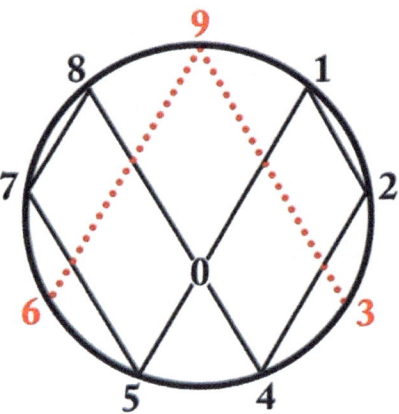

If you take the digits of every result and add them up together, you get 1, 2, 4, 5, 7, and 8, and the circle tends to repeat itself. Hence, the resulting sum will always be 1, 2, 4, 5, 7, and 8. This sequence is infinite and can never be broken, no matter how much you double the numbers. It is a significant sequence as it shows how the energy moves in the universe and can never be destroyed no matter.

You may wonder how the numbers 3, 6, and 9 seem absent in the above answers. This is because the numbers 1, 2, 4, 5, 7, and 8 signify the physical world, whereas 3, 6, and 9 symbolize the divine realm in the physical world. The spiritual world influences the physical world, which means to control any event in the physical universe, you need to decipher the secrets locked in the digits 3, 6, and 9 (often referred to as the 'Tesla Code.')

When you double the numbers 3 and 6, you get the series of 3, 6, 12, 24, 48, etc. When these numbers are added up individually, the resulting number will always be either 3 or 6. You won't find the number 9 anywhere in this sequence, which again seems surprising as it is an essential number in the Tesla Code. Here's the interesting bit. When you double the digit 9, you will always get an answer whose digits, when added up individually, will come out to be 9. The numbers 9, 18, 36, 72, and so on, if broken down into their digits and added, you will get the answer 9. This signifies that the number 9 symbolizes the universe's ultimate power, which can help you control every physical event in this universe if you use it well.

Now that you understand the basics of cymatics and numerology and how the digits 3, 6, and 9 play a considerable role in shaping and functioning the universe, let us explore their relationship with the solfeggio frequencies.

The Solfeggio Frequencies' Link with the Numbers 3, 6 and 9

The solfeggio frequencies are deeply associated with numerology and the numbers 3, 6, and 9. If you individually add up each of the solfeggio frequencies, the outcome would reduce to either 3, 6, or 9. Simply put, all the solfeggio frequencies are divisible by 3, 6, and 9.

The image below shows this for the nine solfeggio frequencies.

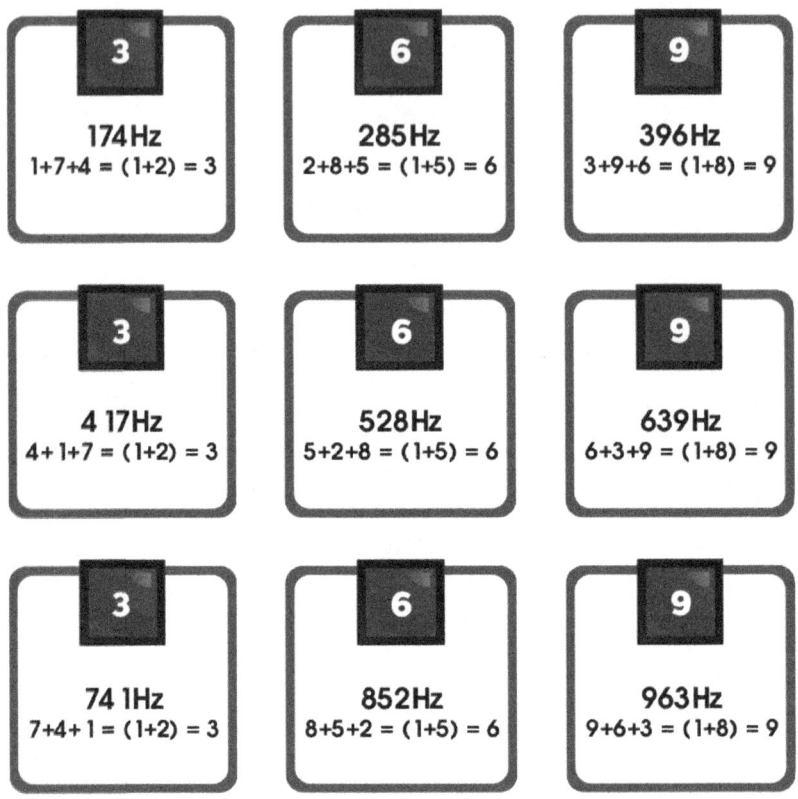

This means that they have the mystical powers of the numbers 3, 6, and 9. Hence, listening to sounds on these frequencies and incorporating them into our lives would undoubtedly produce many healing benefits. Since the numbers 3, 6, and 9 signify the spiritual world and the magnificent power of the universe, anything that operates on these frequencies naturally helps you connect with the universe.

This connection links you with the mighty force of the universe. As you become united with that power, you start to harness its potential and reap its benefits.

It is also essential to understand that numerology is related to your day of birth, and if you figure out your birth code, you can start living a very harmonious life.

Numerology and Your Birth Code

Every aspect of your life revolves around numbers and dates. All these digits have a lot to communicate to us. One such significant number is your birth code which you can derive by adding up all the numbers in your date of birth i.e., day, month, and year. For instance, if you were born on January 1st, 1990, your birth code will be derived as such:

January is the first month, so it has the number 1; your birth date is 1st, so again the number 1; your birth year is 1990, so you will add up 1, 9, 9, and 0 and get 19 which will again be added as 1+9 to accumulate to 10, and finally you add up 1+0 to get 1. Now, you have the numbers 1+1+1, and your answer is 3, which is your birth code.

Every number from 1 to 9 has different strengths, weaknesses, and powers. Let us look at them:

1: It signifies that you believe in being the number 1 in whatever you do, be it running a business, doing a job, etc. You have leadership qualities, and you want to be the best at everything.

2: It symbolizes harmony, love, and compassion; you are likely to be humble and gentle but often more sensitive and emotional than others.

3: It is the number of teamwork, playfulness, self-expression, and generosity. You are likely to be a fun, social person but often opt for shallow pursuits over profound ones that could create a void in your life.

4: This number signifies systematic, planning, and execution which means you are great at planning and organizing things and always want to have relationships with people who are as good as you.

5: This symbolizes freedom and an eagerness to learn, which means you believe in being free, unrestrained, and very passionate. You want someone alongside who lets you fly and explore the world.

6: The number 6 signifies warmth and affection. You are likely to be a loving soul who spreads positivity around and is best suited for careers that help people grow, such as teaching.

7: The number of spirituality, and if 7 is your birth code, you are influenced by your mind and have deep interests in philosophy, favors logic, research, and the deep exploration of ideas.

8: This represents motivation, taking up responsibility, hard work, and fulfilling commitments. You are likely to be someone who believes in working hard and enjoying the yield of your efforts later on.

9: This is the number of humanity and equality. You believe in independence, equality, and rights for everyone and strive towards making it happen for everyone. However, you make sure to take care of your needs first before looking after others.

Now that you have a deeper insight into yourself with your birth code let us further explore the benefits of the solfeggio frequencies and the science behind them in the following chapter.

"If you only knew the magnificence of the 3, 6 and 9, then you would have the key to the universe." - Nikola Tesla

Chapter 3: The Science Behind the Solfeggio Frequencies

Afooter the discovery of the solfeggio, they gained massive popularity. However, by the sixteenth century, the scale was somehow lost. The exact cause behind this issue is unknown to date.

The Theories behind the Loss of Solfeggio Frequencies

Some people believe it was abandoned in exchange for a fresher music scale. In contrast, others strongly believe that it disappeared during Western Europe's religious and political turmoil during the Middle Ages. Many conspiracy theories exist to explain the issue, with a number of them revolving around Roman Catholic Church being responsible for causing the disappearance of the solfeggio frequencies.

During 1800, a constant debate surfaced the entire Europe and America regarding the standardization of music. The frequency at that time kept shifting in between 417 Hz and 470 Hz.

Back in Mozart's time, every instrument that was designed was tuned at a frequency of exactly 432 Hz. Slowly, things evolved at the start of the twentieth century when J. C. Deagan utilized his social connections to change the music industry's frequency completely. It was then that all the musical instruments were tuned at a frequency of 440 Hz. Deagan began lobbying all across Europe and made sure that the 440 Hz frequency became the standard frequency.

In 1935, the Rockefeller foundation gravitated towards adopting the 440 Hz frequency as a means to influence the conscious minds of the people. They wanted to trigger the 'war on the consciousness' with the 440 Hz frequency.

Later, during the era of the Nazis in Germany, it was concluded that all sorts of music must be at a frequency of 440 Hz as this frequency impacts and controls the subconscious aspect of the human mind. The Nazis basically wanted to manipulate the human mind and compel people to think, feel, behave and act only a certain way to achieve their desired objectives.

The Levels of Consciousness

Most people are still unaware that the human mind functions on three levels: conscious, unconscious, and subconscious. The conscious mind is in charge of every action you take fully consciously, such as driving with awareness or consciously cooking.

The unconscious mind serves as your information and memory warehouse as it stocks all the memories you have ever made in your life.

The subconscious mind stores the memories you have just formed and acts more like an arbitrator between the conscious and unconscious states of mind. It picks up all the information stored in your unconscious mind, uses them to create your beliefs and internal program, and then passes on commands to the conscious mind to behave a certain way. This explains why experiences such as bullying and emotional losses during your childhood tend to create insecurities, phobias, and doubts later on in life.

To bring forth any desired change in your personality, you must positively influence your subconscious mind. In fact, the Nazis, and all the people who consciously and tactfully changed the musical world's frequency to 440 Hz, did so with the ulterior motive of taking charge of our subconscious mind.

They were well aware of how we would dance to their tune when our subconscious mind would be in their control via the medium of music. Precisely, this is how Hitler brainwashed an entire nation for many years. And for this very reason, the 440 Hz frequency is often labeled as the 'Luciferian Frequency' or 'Satan's Tone.'

If you have watched the movie 'Kingsman: Secret Service,' you would remember how the character portrayed by Samuel Jackson aims to rule the world by exposing all the people to a particular radio frequency via their cellphones. This is how an average person turns into a malicious gladiator in the movie.

Whatever the exact reason behind the conundrum, the fact is that the solfeggio frequencies did lose their place in the world and were replaced by the popular 'Twelve-Tone Equal Temperament' that comprise the twelve notes of the musical scale used in the music industry today.

To better understand the science and wisdom behind the solfeggio frequencies, aka 'Just Intonation,' it is first essential to comprehend the modern musical scale's effects on our body, mind, and spirit.

How the Twelve-Tone Scale Affect Us

It is crucial to understand the effects of the modern twelve-tone scale on our existence and life to become more motivated to incorporate the solfeggio frequencies in our life. Only when we realize how the modern scale negatively impacts us can we become more driven to explore and practice the solfeggio frequencies.

In Western and classical music, the commonly used tuning system has been the 12 equal temperaments aka the twelve-tone equal temperament (ever since the eighteenth century). It is also referred to as' 12-ET', '12 TET' or 'twelve equal' as it divides the octave on which it lies into twelve parts. All these twelve parts share an equal proportion on the logarithmic scale and have a ratio equivalent to the 12th root of 2, which comes out to be 1.05946.

In modern music, 12-TET is tuned in a manner that stays relative to the standard pitch used in music which has a frequency of 440 Hz and goes by the name of 'A440.' This means the note A is tuned to 440 Hz. The rest of the notes are described as the semitones' multiples, lying either on a lower or higher frequency. The standard pitch, as we discussed earlier, too, was not always 440 Hz. It has gone through many variations in the past.

The 12-TET, while it produces excellent melodies, has quite drastic and undesirable effects on our body, mind, and soul. On a deeper level, it suppresses your emotions, stifles your gut feeling, and limits your level of self-awareness as well as the consciousness of the world around you.

It has also been scientifically proven that the twelve-tone scale is not harmonious with the natural world and the universal forces. It is entirely out of sync with the universe. Anything that does not align with the universal power frequency naturally harms your personality, mood, thoughts, behavior, and life in general.

We are surrounded by some music in our routine lives. From the jingles used in TV ads and digital video commercials to songs played on the radio to the musical tones used in toys and electronics to our phones' ringtones-everything with some hint of music in it is created using the twelve-tone scale.

The more we listen to it, the deeper it imbeds our body and touches us all the way down to our DNA. We complain of how often we experience ailments and problems such as tension, chronic stress, anxiety, depression, chronic pain, fatigue, lethargy, exhaustion, and trauma. What we don't realize is that the 12-TET has something very twisted to do with all these problems.

The table below shows the twelve notes on this modern 12-TET scale along with their respective frequencies:

A	440
B flat	466
B	494
C	523
C sharp	554
D	587
D sharp	622
E	659
F	698
F sharp	740
G	784
A flat	831
A	880

The notes' frequencies on the twelve-tone scale aren't divisible by 3, 6, or 9. The sum of the individual digits of these frequencies becomes any number from 1, 2, 4, 5, 7, and 8, which, as we saw, helps manage the physical world.

The Detrimental Effects of the 12-TET

When something is meant for the material world and not the spiritual world, naturally, it won't yield the desired effects on any element connected to the spiritual world. The human body may be something physical, but it is the heart, mind, and soul that runs it. In this sense, it is a spiritual, mystical element that needs the power, energy, and magical force of the universe to help it exist and function optimally.

This explains why the twelve-tone scale isn't coherent with our mind and soul, which is why listening to anything created using it only negatively affects us and our wellbeing.

The Good News

The good news is that we have the solfeggio frequencies at our disposal to correct the issues triggered by the modern twelve-tone scale. As opposed to the 12-TET, the solfeggio frequencies are created using a perfectly in sync scale with the universe in every way, mainly when studied mathematically. We have proven earlier how each of the nine frequencies is divisible by 3, 6 or 9, and encompass the mystical and healing properties of these numbers- which is why they positively influence our body, mind, and spirit.

From healing emotional trauma to positively altering our DNA to opening your spiritual awareness to fostering happy relationships, the solfeggio scale has brilliant and far-reaching potential.

Many researchers and scientists have studied the healing powers of the solfeggio frequencies, and their findings have more or less been the same. As per an article published in the Anti-Aging Medical News (http://pulsedbiofeedbackclinic.com/wp-content/pdfs/2006_Dec_A4M.pdf) in 2006, it was mentioned how pulsed frequencies (the solfeggio frequencies) cast a very positive influence on osteoporosis, a severe bone condition characterized by weak and brittle bones.

When your body starts to lose too much of its bone structure and loses the capacity to strengthen existing bones or create new bone cells, your bones start to become delicate. In the chronic states of osteoporosis, you may experience bone injury and breakage from minor bumps, falls or even sneezing. While it affects both genders, women are more susceptible to it. However, the article mentioned above proves how solfeggio frequencies may be the perfect antidote to the issue. Since they have phenomenal effects on your DNA, they can help improve the bone structure and heal osteoporosis.

Another study (https://www.researchgate.net/publication/ 309465157_Effect_of_tuning_fork_generated_frequencies_on_ cognition_in_snails_Achatina_fulica) examined the effects of solfeggio frequencies on snails. It was observed that exposure to the solfeggio frequencies positively influenced the snails' brains. The snails who were directly exposed to the solfeggio frequencies became more active, focused, and creative compared to the ones used in the control group of the study.

Moreover, a Japanese study in 2018 studied the stress-reducing powers of the MI-tone of the solfeggio scale, which operates at 528 Hz. It was discovered that the tone had a very positive impact on the human endocrine system. Constant exposure to the frequency helped regulate the hormonal imbalances in the body. As a result, stress-related hormones such as cortisol slowly reduced, which improved the participants' happiness levels. What was even more astonishing was that these effects were observed within just five minutes of exposure to the solfeggio frequencies.

It is crucial to comprehend the relationship between chakras and solfeggio frequencies to grasp how the frequencies work.

Chakras and Solfeggio Frequencies

The universal life force energy, also referred to as 'chi,' 'ki' or 'qi,' is elementary for our survival and wellbeing. When this energy flows smoothly in and out of our body, mind, and spirit, we function in the best way.

The human body comprises around 114 energy channels, aka chakras in Sanskrit. They are constantly spinning vortexes or energy balls that regulate the energy flow in your body. Out of these 114 chakras, 7 are referred to as the major ones. These run from the base of your spine right to the crown of your head.

Due to different life issues such as overthinking, rehashing the painful past, holding grudges, physical ailments, financial troubles, relationship problems, spiritual matters, and the likes, sometimes energy gets blocked in multiple ways, even in all of the chakras. It is also possible that some of the chakras may have never been opened and activated to allow energy to flow from them evenly.

Whether a chakra is closed or struggling with an energy blockage, it does not work optimally as long as these two issues are present. Whatever problem you are facing in life continues to worsen as long as the chakras aren't fixed. We may blame the problem on external factors, poor health, or our own inabilities, but we don't realize that they stem from energy imbalances and blockages.

Since these chakras are constantly vibrating vortexes, it is understandable how they have a particular frequency. Anything that complements their frequency helps activate, rehabilitate and align them. This is where solfeggio frequencies come in handy.

Different solfeggio frequencies complement different chakras and restore harmony to them with their energy vibrations. Once the chakra is relieved of energy congestion, it starts to function smoothly, and your life gets back on track.

Sometime around 1952, Winfried Otta Schumann, a renowned physicist of German origin, worked on documenting the electromagnetic resonances between the Earth's surface and the ionosphere- the region of Earth's atmosphere charged by electric ions.

Schumann found out that lightning produced a discharge that then created electromagnetic waves. These waves resonated at very low-frequency ranges varying between 7.86 Hz and 8 Hz. He referred to this frequency as the 'heartbeat of Earth.' Since Schumann coined the term, this frequency is also known as 'Schumann resonance.'

After Schumann, researcher, and doctoral candidate 'Herbert Konig' furthered Schumann's research. He extensively worked on the Schumann resonances and discovered that they complemented different human brain activity levels. He concluded by comparing the human brain's EEG recordings with the electromagnetic fields rising from the Earth.

He also found out that these resonances corresponded to

the five diverse brainwave states: gamma, beta, alpha, theta, and delta. The brainwaves are basically electrical impulses created in your brain. Your thoughts, feelings, emotions, attitudes, and behaviors are communicated within your brain between the different neurons (brain cells). All the brainwaves are created through the synchronized electrical pulses given off by masses of neurons, all trying to communicate with one another. The brainwaves occur at different times of the day as we engage in various activities from sleeping to learning to playing to actively thinking, etc.

Research (https://www.ncbi.nlm.nih.gov/pubmed/26785376) on the subject revealed a more profound association between the human brain's activity and the Schumann resonance. Moreover, it has also been proven that Schumann resonance offers better synchronization for optimal brain functioning. (https://www.sciencedirect.com/science/article/abs/pii/S0306987703000276) Now you may be thinking of the connection between the Schumann resonances and Solfeggio frequencies.

Besides clearing the energy blockages in the chakras, the solfeggio frequencies produce harmony in your body as they resonate with the Schumann resonance of 8 Hz. These waves are extracted by frequencies starting at 8 Hz going all the way up till the C note starts to vibrate at a frequency of 256 Hz. The A note begins to vibrate at a frequency of 432 Hz. When music harmonizes with this frequency, it is known as 'scientific tuning.' This is another reason why the solfeggio frequencies promote healing and calming effects in the body, allowing you to break free of physical, mental, emotional, and spiritual problems.

With the foundations covered, let us now explore each of the nine solfeggio frequencies, one by one, in the chapters to come to discover their splendor better. Prior to that, let us take a look at their inner healing powers.

"If you want to find the secrets of the universe, think in terms of energy, frequency, and vibration." — Nikola Tesla

Chapter 4: Solfeggio Frequencies And Inner Healing Numbers 1-9

Solfeggio frequencies bring about massive inner healing in your body, spirit, and mind. Their effects are magical, but it is only with practice and consistency that you can reap those benefits.

Inner Healing with Solfeggio Frequencies

When you break down the digits of each of the nine solfeggio frequencies and add them up together, you get a single digit. Each of those nine individual digits, in the end, is linked with a certain aspect of inner healing. The table below shows you how to reach that individual digit for every solfeggio frequency as well as the kind of inner healing and comfort that frequency brings about in you:

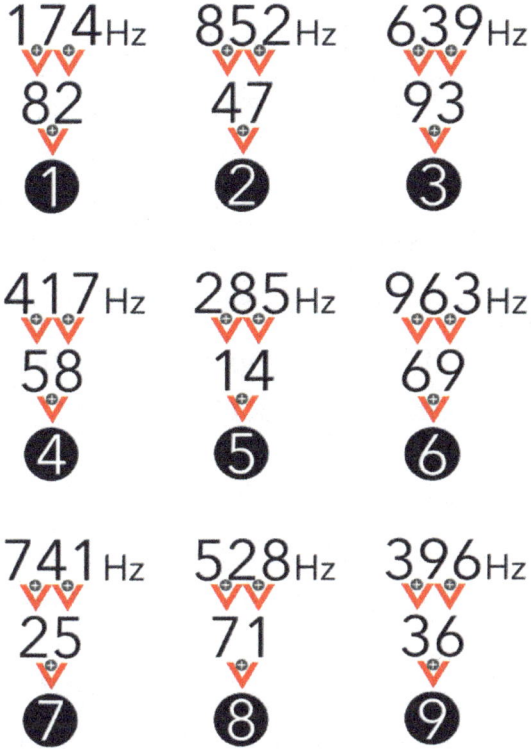

Numerology Vibrations - Calculation Chart

With the above method of calculations, the 9 solfeggio frequencies each has a number from 1-9. From how the numbers are calculated, the numerology vibration forms in each of the solfeggio frequencies.

I have interpreted all the 9 numerology vibrations from the numbers.

One can use these numerology vibrations to examine their own inner or hidden energy.

1. 174 Hz- 82- 1 , Inner Personality

This frequency, when broken down, comes down to the

number 82-1, which is linked with your inner personality. This means that by listening to this frequency, you can bring about massive changes to your personality. Try it here (https://
youtu.be/RJwZE7Peocc)

You can let go of your inner hesitance, personal limitations, and everything that holds you back from being you.

Quite often in life, it so happens that we feel an urge to do something, to bring about a change, but something from within ourselves prohibits us from taking that leap of faith. This boils down to a lack of inner strength to believe in yourself and follow your intuition. You want to live the life of your dreams. You want to be limitless, and you want nothing to stop you from getting what you deserve, be it a great relationship, the business empire you wish to set up, or building a strong spiritual connection with the higher force you believe in. All of that can happen if you let go of the inner kinks that hold you back, and the 174 Hz frequency helps you do the job nicely.

2. 852 Hz- 47- 2 , Character Perception

47-2 When broken down to a single digit, this frequency comes down to the number 2, which is linked with character perception. In the field of social psychology, 'person/ character perception' encompasses the different mental processes we make use of to create the various impressions of people around us and even ourselves. This refers to how we form those impressions and the conclusions we create about them which are centered on our impressions.

We make judgments about people all the time, from the new co-worker who just joined the firm to the mail delivery guy who came with package delivery to a friend that we have known for years. Similarly, based on how we perceive ourselves, we create a character perception of our own image. This character perception directly impacts our self-esteem and self-confidence. If your character perception of yourself is of a strong, confident person who positively impacts others, you naturally feel good about yourself. However, it can be of a confident person in the negative sense, and you may realize your ability to overpower and dominate others and feel good about it. In this sense, your character perception is negative and keeps you from bringing about inner healing.

Another unhealthy angle of character perception is when you consider yourself weak and completely flawed. This type of perception obstructs your self-belief and hinders you from unleashing your true power. To become unstoppable and heal yourself in a manner that allows you to unlock your true potential and use it to do good in the world, you need to have a very balanced and positive character perception.

In addition, you also need to inculcate the ability to be non-judgmental towards others. When we form character perceptions of others, we are mostly putting labels on people we don't really know or may not be aware of all aspects of their lives in case we know them. This keeps us from knowing people well and being kind to them.

The 852 Hz and its power rooted in the number 2 allow you to break these shackles and create the ability to form a positive character perception of yourself and others, which ultimately allows you to correct your personality flaws and do better in the world. If your birth date corresponds to the number 2, this is the solfeggio frequency you need to listen to frequently so you can let go of the judgmental behavior you display for others, and even yourself. As you let go of meaningless judgments, you realize how much you have to offer to the world around you, and find yourself developing into a more confident being. Try the frequency here. (https://youtu.be /aJ2gDWirnYU)

3. 639 Hz- 93- 3 , Emotional Triggers

The 683 Hz frequency is associated with the powerful number '3.' The number 93-3 brings about inner healing through balancing your emotions and responding better to emotional triggers.

At some point in our lives, almost all of us have reacted irrationally to our emotions. This could be in the form of venting out your frustrations at the wrong people, taking uninformed and hasty decisions, judging people, and jumping too quickly to certain emotions to create mountains out of molehills. Our emotions influence us to a great degree, so building emotional intelligence is critical if we are to live a harmonious life. The number 3 allows you to do that by bringing forth balance and stability in your emotions.

Suppose you regularly listen to the solfeggio frequency of 639 Hz. In that case, you will still experience a range of different emotions at different times in your life, and as per diverse situations you encounter, but you will learn to manage your reactions to them. Instead of jumping to the gun, you will take time to settle in with your emotions, embrace them and then find the right way to respond to them.

Learning the art of managing emotional triggers brings forth massive freedom in your life. You feel calmer because you know you can control yourself, and once you can put a leash on your emotions, you find it easier to do what feels right for yourself. It is not that you won't experience any intense emotions in life after using this solfeggio frequency. It is just that it will allow you to have a better grip on them. Before reacting to an emotion, you will understand how to best process it, and then use it in the most constructive manner so you leverage the power of emotions instead of allowing them to wreak havoc inside of you. Try the frequency here. (https://youtu.be/dYSMvjGpXMo)

4. 417 Hz- 58-4 , Hidden Traits

When the frequency of 417 Hz is broken down to 58-4, it comes down to the single-digit of '4', so it is associated with the power of number 4, which is to help you explore and unlock your hidden traits.

All of us have a lot more potential than we give ourselves credit for, but the reason why we struggle to give that due credit is because we aren't really aware of those potentials. You may have the potential to be a great public speaker, but you have been scared of speaking in crowds all your life, which is why you don't really explore that side of you and never really discover it. Thriving in life is directly linked to self-discovery. You need to keep exploring yourself to discover more about your likes, dislikes, interests, talents, aspirations, inner calling, and the likes. Unless you introspect, you won't truly find out what you are good at, what you are meant to do in life, and the right direction you are to steer into.

Not just that, but self-discovery is also about finding your strong and weak suits. Perhaps, you feel an inner resistance to pursue your ambitions, and you don't realize that it is rooted in your anger management issues. Sometimes, we need more than just sitting with ourselves in solitude to find our latent traits and talents, and this is where the solfeggio frequency of 417 Hz serves its purpose. It allows you to know who you are by kick-starting the self-discovery process that continues for the rest of your life.

You start to make great realizations about yourself that lead to massive self-awareness. The more you understand yourself, the better you learn about what you wish to do and how to bring about that change, and that's exactly how you change your life for the better. You can try the 417 Hz frequency here. (https://youtu.be/g4UtY228AGM)

5. 285 Hz- 14- 5 , Arbitrary Behaviors

The 285 Hz frequency boils down to the number 5, 14-5 which is associated with arbitrary behavior. It brings about inner healing in yourself by helping you recognize and correct the different arbitrary behaviors you may experience in routine life.

Arbitrary is something determined by a whim or a judgment and not really based on any rule of thumb or logical reasoning. Arbitrary behavior is a kind of conduct you practice without any rationality associated with it.

For instance, you may find yourself losing your temper at people who haven't wronged you, or you may go out of your way to help people who don't deserve that special treatment.

Understanding the different arbitrary behaviors you engage in is crucial because this knowledge helps you realize where, when, and how you go wrong and the measures you need to practice to better those behaviors. The 285 solfeggio frequency can be of enormous help. Listening to it helps you explore and recognize your arbitrary behaviors and slowly replace them with improved and rational ones. You realize how you resort to exhibiting arbitrary behaviors, how they are unconstructive to you, and find ways to manage them effectively. You can try this 285 Hz frequency. (https://youtu.be/e-0Ic2hpgEQ)

6. 963 Hz- 69- 6 , Crisis Reaction

The 963 Hz frequency is associated with the power of the number 69-6, which is for crisis reaction. All of us go through many different crises in our lives. From relationship problems to financial instability to struggling with bankruptcy to the inability to find your inner voice and a sense of purpose to feeling inadequate to mid-life crisis to existential crises, and several other problems- some crisis always comes our way, and often when we least expect it.

How we handle those crises and manage our emotions in those turbulent times speaks a lot about how well we do in life. Crisis management goes a step further than having emotional intelligence. Of course, you need to be emotionally intelligent and secure to handle challenges well in life. Still, you also need to have good analytical, problem solving, and decision-making skills for excellent crisis management. Regularly listening to the 963 Hz frequency helps you build great crisis management skills that call for extraordinary improvements in life.

The 963 Hz solfeggio frequency helps you assess things objectively, analyze the pros and cons of different options, weigh them against each other, and opt for the most beneficial solution during a crisis. It does that by calming your volatile emotions, and helping you control your ability to jump to conclusions instantly. You can try the 963 Hz frequency here. (https://youtu.be/8_yCzcU4fwo)

7. 741 Hz- 25- 7 , Change Adaptability

This solfeggio frequency, when broken down, 25-7 comes out to the digit 7 and is associated with the power of 'change adaptability.' Change in life is the only constant. Nothing remains the same and is bound to change.

However, not all of us have a very positive and accepting attitude towards change. Many of us struggle to experience growth and improvement because we keep resisting changes and challenges in life. Not all changes are necessarily negative; some might be positive, but we can only learn that if we are receptive to the idea of change and evolving ourselves with those changes. The 741 Hz frequency allows you to improve yourself by slowly improving your ability to receive and accept change positively.

The more you listen to it, the more you become open to the idea of experiencing changes in life and find yourself handling them positively. It is only when you embrace change that you learn to use it to your advantage. You may have opposed many changes to date, some of which could have been great opportunities in disguise. Since resisting change comes easy to us, we let go of chances that may actually be advantageous to us. However, the 741 Hz frequency changes this for the better by opening your mind to the possibility of experimenting with new ideas, embracing change, and propelling yourself further towards growth in unprecedented situations. Here is the 741 Hz frequency. (https://youtu.be/q3YRTZGKx8Q)

8. 528 Hz- 71- 8 , Exploited Response

When broken down to an individual digit, this frequency comes down to the number '8', which is linked to exploited response. Sometimes, we tend to develop manipulative and exploitative behaviors that may help us achieve some ulterior motives but aren't healthy, to begin with.

Perhaps, you have the tendency to dominate insecure people around you and enjoy having an overpowering effect on them. While you may not realize the grim consequences of such behaviors on their life, you should know that exploiting people ends up often ruining their wellbeing.

On the other hand, you may be the victim of exploitation at the hands of someone else in your life too. If you allow people to subdue you and misuse you, you turn into a pushover who loses self-respect with time. You surely don't want to go down that rabbit hole, right?

In that sense, you need to harness the power of the solfeggio frequency of 528 Hz as it helps soothe and overcome such behaviors allowing you to become a better, well-rounded person. Listening to 528 Hz helps you understand your exploitative behaviors as well as those of the people around you. You get to the root cause of your manipulative behaviors, and learn to tame them down. Plus, you also become confident enough to stand up for yourself when the need be so you keep your power within your control instead of giving it to others. Try it here. (https://youtu.be/-VOOwI4Ufpo)

9. 396 Hz- 36- 9 , Ambition Attitude

The solfeggio frequency of 396 Hz boils down to the number 36-9 associated with the 'ambition attitude.' Thriving in life is largely dependent on how ambitious you are and how well you are aware of your ambitions. While some of us are aware of our aspirations from a young age, not all of us have that awareness.

Additionally, some of us who may be aware of our ambitions may not always have that ambitious attitude to pursue them and use them to bring about meaningful change in our lives. We complain of how our lives lack meaning often, but we struggle to realize that the issue may be rooted in the lack of an ambitious attitude. This is where this frequency comes in handy.

It removes the many inner barriers that keep you from exploring your ambitions and building the ambition attitude, so you know what you want and find in yourself the courage to pursue your passions. Naturally, when you ambitiously follow suit of where your heart takes you, your feel empowered from within, and your life gains structure. More importantly, you start digging into your thoughts, desires and feelings to better understand your most genuine needs and aspirations. Quite often, we aren't even aware of those, and it is only when we better understand our ambitions that we figure out what our heart desires the most in this life. Try the 396 Hz frequency here. (https://youtu.be/pyz7oc8zcqk)

As you can see, solfeggio frequencies are quite magical. All our lives, we think of something extraordinary to change everything for the better. Little did we think that power would come in the form of beats and frequencies.

There is more to these frequencies besides their inner healing capabilities. To truly understand the magic locked in solfeggio frequencies, it is important to dig into their names and characteristics. We have discussed earlier how each of these frequencies has certain powers locked in them.

With the basics covered, let us now delve into the specific details of different solfeggio frequencies, what they can do for you, and how you can use them on a regular basis to bring about the desired changes in your life.

In the chapters to follow, we will discuss each of the solfeggio frequencies individually along with their characteristics and their powers to change your life for the better starting from the note UT with the 396 Hz frequency.

"Numbers constitute the only universal language."
— Nathanael West

Chapter 5: UT- 396 Hz- Releasing Fear and Guilt

L et us begin this journey by discussing the UT note with a frequency of 396 Hz. This note is believed to provide permanent relief from grief, transform agony into happiness, and liberate you from insecurities, fear, and guilt.

UT Tone and Grief Relief

The first note of the 'Just Intonation' is UT that vibrates at 396 Hz. This frequency is often associated with assuaging feelings of discomfort, grief, and guilt in your mind that you tend to accumulate over the years.

Frequently, we experience inner friction that keeps us from moving on in life. We feel disturbed from within, lack self-confidence, and feel guilty about the many mistakes we made in our past. Instead of moving past them, we hold onto them, consequently nurturing grudges against ourselves. Such emotions and feelings create toxicity inside of us that keeps us from feeling peaceful.

It is crucial to clear such energies from your subconscious mind, so you start to let go of your fears, self-doubts and guilt, and find it easy to accept the past as a bygone to move ahead in life.

By listening to sounds at the 396 Hz frequency, you expose your mind to calming energy that clears away all sorts of negativities from your subconscious mind. You gradually make your peace with your past, stop feeling remorseful and embrace the present moment.

The UT note also helps you escape from fear and guilt by clearing away energy congestions in the root chakra. Let us dig deeper into this aspect.

UT Note and Root Chakra

The root chakra is the first of the seven major chakras in the human body. It rests at the base of your spine, right in the tailbone area. It vibrates at a frequency of 396 Hz and is associated with the color' red.'

White light is composed of seven colors. When it disperses, white light breaks down into its constituent colors: red, orange, yellow, green, blue, indigo and violet. This happens when white light is absorbed by your body as well. As it separates into its seven-colored components, every chakra absorbs a particular color corresponding to its respective frequency. Since the color red and root chakra vibrate at the same frequency, the two complement each other well.

The root chakra goes by the name *Muladhara* in Sanskrit, which means 'root chakra.' This chakra governs your foundation for life by providing you with the ability to feel anchored to the present moment, be emotionally stable, and withstand challenges in life with strength and grit. It also helps you enjoy a sense of stability and security in life.

When the Muladhara is inactive or blocked, the blockage manifests itself in the shape of issues such as constipation, arthritis, colon problems, bladder issues, low self-esteem, feeling insecure, and struggling with financial instability. The feelings of insecurity, plow self-esteem, and struggling to feel stable in life are also associated with our tendency to hold onto past grievances and not moving on.

Once all the different energy blockages in the root chakra clear away, energy starts to flow in and out of it smoothly, and the chakra operates optimally. Gradually, you feel connected to yourself, begin to feel grounded to the present moment, release all sorts of guilt and fear from your subconscious, and feel emotionally stable.

We mentioned above how the 396 Hz frequency does the same. Hence, can effectively use it to activate and restore harmony to the root chakra.

To achieve this goal, here is how you can incorporate the 396 Hz frequency in your life.

Healing Yourself with 396 Hz Frequency

You can do this by:

- You can listen to instrumental music and any musical piece with a frequency of 396 Hz. You can find many such musical pieces online, including this one (https://youtu.be/pyz7oc8zcqk) with a very soothing and serene vibe, and instantly makes you feel peaceful.

- Listen to sounds and music on this frequency as often as possible, at least for 5 to 10 minutes daily. Start your day listening to beats on 396 Hz, and spend a few minutes tuning into the music whenever you feel emotionally disturbed or struggle with agony.

- To enhance the sounds' effectiveness, listen to them in a calming, peaceful environment that promotes relaxation in your body and mind. You could set up a corner in your house as your calming or meditation spot. Clear it off any clutter, tidy it up and decorate it with fresh plants, wall art, or anything that symbolizes peace. Spend a few minutes in the spot listening to one or more solfeggio frequencies to heal yourself. This practice will be the same for healing through all the other frequencies, so ensure to observe it every time you listen to a beat operating on solfeggio frequencies.

- Since the 396 Hz frequency heals the root chakra, close your eyes and locate the Muladhara spot (right at the root of your spine) while listening to the music. Once you identify it, imagine red-colored light entering the site, slowly growing bigger and brighter and spreading to the entire body to liberate it of all sorts of negativity. Work on this practice for 5 to 10 minutes daily to slowly heal your root chakra. Once it stabilizes, you automatically feel free, light, and grounded in life.

Consistency and commitment are two crucial C's to observe to get compound results in any aspect of life. The same applies to heal yourself through solfeggio frequencies. Ensure to spend a few minutes of your day listening to beats at a specific solfeggio frequency. It is best to start from the first note and slowly scale up, and once you have spent about a total of two to three months listening to all the solfeggio frequencies, you can spend more time listening to a certain one that relates the most to your current problems.

However, if you are currently well aware of your exact issue and wish to heal it first, start with the frequency corresponding to that. For instance, if you want to mend a broken relationship in your life, and that's the most pressing concern in your life at the moment, start by listening to beats at 639 Hz frequency first, and you can work on the remaining ones later on.

Let us now move to the subsequent frequency of the tone 'RE' to explore its healing effects on your spirit, mind, and body.

"Everything in Life is Vibration" – Albert Einstein

Chapter 6: RE- 417 Hz- Undoing Problems in Life and Facilitating Change

The second solfeggio frequency is the tone RE that vibrates at a frequency of 417 Hz and brings about positive changes in your life, helping you settle with the many changes life brings forth towards you. Let us talk more about it in this chapter.

The RE Note and How it Facilitates Change in Life

The frequency of 417 Hz is referred to as the frequency of renewal and change in life. Just like fear and guilt tend to obstruct our growth and prosperity in life, so do the different traumatic experiences we go through. Even if we walk ahead of those turbulent episodes, somehow, their impression stays afresh in our subconscious mind. These impressions keep creating hurdles in our routine functioning as well as our ability to stay happy.

To overcome the issue, you need the help of the RE tone. Like how water waves wash over the seashore, the RE tone vibrating at 417 Hz clears off all the debris left over by painful memories and any negative energy you have picked up during the day.

Often, certain situations tend to weigh us down because we fail to analyze them from positive perspectives. This issue boils down to our inability to think clearly and with an optimistic attitude. The 417 Hz frequency cleanses our body, mind, and spirit of these toxic energies and beliefs. As you get rid of them, you find it easier to perceive everything with a fresh mind, soul, and eyes, which broadens your horizons and ability to analyze different situations and live a happy life.

RE Note and Sacral Chakra

The second chakra, aka the sacral chakra, is referred to as *Svadhisthana* in Sanskrit. It is situated right beneath your navel and is linked with the color' orange.' It is in charge of governing your creative and sexual energy. Moreover, it is associated with how you understand and manage your emotions and those of others, so in a way, it regulates and shapes your emotional intelligence (EI.)

Whenever energy is obstructed in the sacral chakra, it manifests itself in the form of different emotional and physical ailments. Physical issues related to the sacral chakra include infections in the urinary tract, impotence, and chronic back pains.

Emotional problems pertaining to the energy blockages and imbalances in the sacral chakra include feeling worthless. Moreover, since this chakra regulates your creative and sexual abilities, you tend to struggle to express yourself creatively and sexually with your intimate partners whenever it is blocked.

You can experience creative thinking problems, have a narrow sense of perspective, and cannot think outside the box to solve different problems in your life. Also, your libido either becomes too low or too high. Either you find it hard to function sexually or become obsessed with it. Since extremity in any scenario is bad, the extremes of both, a high or low libido, negatively affect your life.

Since the sacral chakra vibrates at 417 Hz, you can easily heal it with the 417 Hz solfeggio frequency. The serene vibes of the 417 Hz beat of RE release all sorts of energy blockages from your sacral chakra and slowly align it, improving your creative abilities, sexual drive, and ability to understand and manage your emotions and consequently all the physical ailments you are going through.

Here is how you can use the 417 Hz frequency to fix your sacral chakra and the issues that stem from it.

How to Use the 417 Hz Frequency

Get started with undoing all the problems in your life and becoming open to different life changes with the following practices:

- Look up some catchy tunes on the 417 frequency like this one (https://youtu.be/g4UtY228AGM) here which I have prepared. Listening to it daily for 5 to 10 minutes is beneficial. Sit in your meditation/ calming spot as taught in the previous chapter. However, it is not mandatory to always listen to the solfeggio frequency there. You can do it wherever you want and at any time of the day.

- To quickly heal your sacral chakra with the 417 Hz frequency, listen to beats created on it whenever possible. If you are driving, play the tune; put on your headphones and listen to the beat as you work on an assignment; use it as background music when friends or loved ones are over at your place- it has a very calming feel which will soothe everyone's stressed nerves.

- Whenever possible, close your eyes when listening to the 417 Hz frequency and imagine a warm orange ball of light gently entering the spot of your sacral chakra and gently heating it in the process. As it warms your sacral chakra, the chakra starts to light up, and with that, every ounce of energy congestion clears from it. Imagine the orange light glowing brighter in intensity, slowly dissipating to the rest of your body to heal it of all sorts of energy imbalances.

Take out a few minutes of your routine for this practice daily, and soon you will notice massive improvements in your mood, creativity, and physical ailments.

Let us now move to the third kind of solfeggio frequency and the chakra it corresponds to.

"Music can heal the wounds which medicine cannot touch."– Debasish Mridha

Chapter 7: MI- 528 HZ- DNA Repair and Transformation in Life

The third solfeggio frequency is of the tone Mi which runs on a frequency of 528 Hz, divisible by the number 6. Let us explore more of its healing abilities in this chapter.

MI Brings Forth Massive Transformation in Life

The word 'mi' is derived from the word *Mira Gestorum* of Latin origin, which translates to 'miracle.' The power of MI is that it brings forth extraordinary and remarkable transformation in your life. While you may think this transformation is just limited to your sense of awareness, the reality is MI does the trick by influencing both your DNA and consciousness.

DNA refers to the molecule carrying your genetic code. It contains all your biological information pertinent to yourself. Everything from eye color to your height to your health and your likelihood of acquiring health problems is imprinted on your DNA.

While you can bring about different personality changes by working on it, your DNA makeup is beyond your control. This is what man has always believed. However, with solfeggio frequencies, this realization advanced up a level too. It was observed that listening to solfeggio frequencies, particularly that of MI can bring about tremendous changes in your DNA's composition, which helps you get rid of any abnormalities or problems in your genetic makeup that threaten your wellbeing and survival.

When your DNA arrangement transforms for the better, it is a miracle of sorts that enhances your life quality. Moreover, the 528 Hz frequency activates your ability to think clearly and rationally. This clarity triggers a change of peace in your life and also boosts your creative faculties. With all these changes in your life, you find it easy to love yourself and enjoy life. This is why the 528 Hz is also referred to as the *'love frequency.'*

Besides, the MI tone also clarifies all sorts of energy obstructions in the solar plexus chakra. Let us discuss the relationship of the two below.

MI and Solar Plexus Chakra

The solar plexus chakra goes by the name *Manipura* in Sanskrit and rests in your stomach. It is responsible for shaping and improving your sense of self-esteem, self-confidence, and self-worth in life, which means it primarily affects your ability to control your life and its quality. It is linked to the color yellow.

In case energy is logged up in the solar plexus chakra, you struggle with self-esteem and self-confidence issues. Either your self-esteem drops to exceedingly low levels, or it balloons up to the extent that you start to turn into a narcissist. Either way, it harms your wellbeing as well as relationships with your loved ones.

When your self-esteem is strained, you lack self-belief, which keeps you from pursuing your aspirations and living life on your terms. You find it easy to give in to others' demands and serve more like their personal puppet. On the other hand, with an inflated sense of self-esteem, you become self-obsessed to the extent that you fail to see anyone and anything beyond yourself and end up hurting others in the process.

Moreover, energy jamming up in the solar plexus chakra also represents itself in physical issues, including indigestion, eating disorders, digestive problems, heartburn, and ulcers. Since the Manipura is the chakra of your personal power, it keeps you from realizing and channelizing your true potential when it undergoes any blockage or is inactive.

Both the Manipura and the color orange vibrate at 528 Hz-similar to the MI tone. For this very reason, listening to the 528 Hz frequency promotes transformational healing in the solar plexus chakra. As all the different kinds of blockages and issues associated with it clear, you can now harness your power and transform yourself and your life for the better, which along with DNA repair, is a huge miracle.

Let us now take a look at how you can bring about this transformation in your life.

How to Use the 528 Hz Frequency

Start with these practices to fix genetic problems and your life for good:

- One of the best ways to benefit from the power of 528 Hz frequency is to listen to a corresponding note daily, at least for 10 minutes. You can try this one here. (https://youtu.be/-VOOwI4Ufpo)
- It may feel slightly irritating at first, primarily because you have to listen to a 'beeping' tone for about 5 to 10 minutes- which can be annoying. That said, I encourage you to go ahead with it nonetheless. Just think of how this practice would restore complete harmony in your body, mind, and soul and help you advance to a whole new level of clarity. Imagine living your best life to date, and listen to the tune while picturing yourself being completely happy, successful, wealthy, abundant, or however, you wish to be. Looking at the bigger picture motivates you to stick to the practice for the long haul.
- When you listen to the MI tone, fix your attention on the spot of your solar plexus chakra and visualize loving, yellow-colored energy stirring up inside your abdomen and gradually engulfing your entire abdomen and then your whole body in itself. As the power grows bigger and stronger, it spreads to every inch and part of your body and heals all sorts of impurities and issues in it.

It is recommended that you envision yellow light healing your solar plexus chakra whenever you listen to the solfeggio frequency of 528 Hz, but it is not obligatory. You can easily listen to the tune even while doing routine chores, as closing your eyes and always picturing the yellow healing energy isn't always possible.

With that, we now move on to the fourth solfeggio frequency in the following chapter of this book.

"Sound will be the medicine of the future." — *Edgar Cayce*

Chapter 8: FA- 639 Hz- Reconnects You to Yourself and Balances Your Relationships

The fourth solfeggio frequency is of the note FA that vibrates on the 639 Hz frequency. It, too, possesses extraordinary powers that can rehabilitate your life to a great extent. Let us know more about it here.

FA is the Tone of Relationships and Connection

The 639 Hz frequency is divisible by 9, hence encompasses the extraordinary powers of the number 9. This frequency is referred to as the tone of relationships, harmony, and connection. FA brings about a massive transformation in your life concerning yourself and all the other people you are connected to.

Friction in life often stems from two core reasons: lack of connection and compassion for yourself and feeling disconnected from your loved ones. This is when you struggle to feel comfortable with yourself and build loving, happy relationships with people you feel close to or want to get close to. Naturally, when you lack love for yourself and your loved ones, life feels meaningless and incomplete.

FA has the magnificent power to smooth out any sort of

rockiness you experience in your relationships, as well as any kind of disconnect you have for yourself. For these reasons, FA is also known as *the frequency of sympathy, social connections, understanding, mutual respect,* and *tolerance.*

The heart chakra also regulates all of these functions and elements and vibrates at the 639 Hz frequency, so the FA tone is perfect for aligning the heart chakra. Let us dig deeper into the association of these two here.

Heart Chakra and the 639 Hz Frequency

The heart chakra is the fourth of the seven critical chakras. It is referred to as *Anahata* in Sanskrit and is located just in the middle of the chest. Considering its name and position, it comes as no surprise that this chakra governs the physical and emotional aspects of your heart and is about your ability and capacity to express compassion and affection for yourself as well as others around you.

The heart chakra is associated with a green light that vibrates at the 639 Hz frequency. Any misalignment in the heart chakra manifests itself through physical issues such as heart problems, weight management issues, and breathing problems such as asthma.

Moreover, energy congestion in the heart chakra also brings about many emotional and psychological issues in your life. Often, these blockages keep you from clearly expressing your love for yourself and others. You may have self-acceptance issues that refrain you from being comfortable in your skin and loving yourself just the way you are. Besides, you may also find it hard to show your love to others, express your sentiments to them and give as well as receive love from them.

These energy blockages can result in two extremes in this scenario too. Either you become too giving towards others to the extent that you disregard your wellbeing entirely and turn into a people pleaser or become utterly obsessed with yourself and see nobody beyond yourself. In both scenarios, you often feel alone, insecure, and hurt because people mistreat people-pleasers or distance themselves from those who fail to care for them.

While these problems are grim and quite detrimental to your wellbeing, they come with just the right solution-healing with the 639 Hz solfeggio frequency.

How to Heal Yourself with the 639 Hz Frequency

Get started with the following techniques to restore perfect harmony to your heart chakra and overall wellbeing:

- Begin by looking up some soothing 639 Hz tunes online. Here (https://youtu.be/dYSMvjGpXMo) is one for you that has a very reassuring and sedative vibe to it. Start by listening to it for 3 to 5 minutes daily and gradually increasing the duration of the practice. Every time you want to trigger a state of trance and tranquility, hit up this tone and allow yourself to relax in a comforting state of mind.
- Try to do routine chores with this tune in the background to train your subconscious mind to slowly accept the melody and use it to clear away energy imbalances in your body, mind, and spirit.

- Set a time of the day, at least thrice every week, and devote about 5 to 10 minutes to meditate using this tune. Sit or lie down comfortably, preferably in your meditation/ calming corner or anywhere if you are outside. Once settled, close your eyes gently and locate your heart chakra in the middle of your chest. If you want, place your hand on it and picture a beautiful, calming, green-colored light entering your heart and softly growing bigger in size and intensity. As it becomes brighter and more prominent in magnitude, envision it spreading all around your heart and then slowly encapsulating every inch of your body in its glow.

- Focus on your breath, and imagine the green light clearing away all sorts of toxicities from your heart chakra and your entire body with it.

- Whenever possible, picture yourself feeling happy and peaceful while listening to a beat on the 639 Hz frequency. Think of how you envision being your happiest self. Reflect on the kind of relationships you would want in life then and the people you imagine or wish to be surrounded by. Picture this scenario as you listen to the soothing tune to manifest it as your reality gradually.

- Remember, the human mind cannot distinguish between what's real and imaginary. It accepts whatever you feed to it with conviction, clarity, and consistency. So if you constantly give yourself suggestions on how happy you feel, surrounded by loving relationships, your mind believes it as the truth and then makes you work accordingly to make it happen for real.

A conviction with consistency is the key to achieving your desired goals, so practice these measures regularly, and very soon, you will cleanse your life of any sort of hatred and disconnect. You will also fall in love with yourself and others while getting genuine love from them in exchange.

Let us now move to the next frequency in line.

"Nothing rests; everything moves; everything vibrates."
– The Kybalion

Chapter 9: SOL- 741 Hz- Solves Problems and Improves Self-Expression

The fifth solfeggio frequency is that of SOL that functions on 741 Hz. If you add up these numbers together, the outcome is 3, which means SOL possesses the life-changing powers of the number 3. Let us dig right into this frequency in this chapter.

SOL Solves Your Life's Problems by Enhancing Your Self-Expression

At the fifth solfeggio frequency, we land at 741 Hz. This frequency is a tone of solving different problems pertinent to yourself and your life, mainly those that steam from your inability to express your voice openly and comfortably.

One of the innate human needs is to be heard and voice your concerns to everyone. When you struggle with expressing your thoughts, ideas, and feelings, you experience an ill feeling from within. This may be rooted in the complete inability to express yourself to others or lack of strength to speak with complete honesty. When such problems arise, you do not express your feelings to others, convey your concerns to them, and struggle to build meaningful relationships.

Moreover, if you cannot speak with authenticity, you may adopt a superficial demeanor. You are likely to portray yourself as someone you are not, which you are not comfortable with from within. Plus, there is always the scare of exposing your true self being which comes with the tension of being alienated from your loved ones.

The 741 Hz frequency provides freedom from all these problems by freeing you of all sorts of emotional restrictions and issues with expressing yourself. It removes all the harmful electromagnetic radiation and toxins from your body, especially those that keep you from speaking clearly, honestly, and comfortably. With these issues eradicated, your life becomes emotionally stable.

Also, the SOL note aligns your throat chakra, which brings about more harmony in your life.

SOL and the Throat Chakra

This is the fifth of the seven major chakras and sits in your throat. Considering its name and its relation with the 741 Hz frequency, it is understandable how it governs your ability to communicate and express yourself verbally.

The throat chakra is associated with the color blue that resonates with the 741 Hz frequency. It is known as *Vishuddha* in Sanskrit and governs your throat and all sorts of physical and emotional issues pertinent to it.

If you have a closed or blocked Vishuddha, you will likely experience problems linked to your gums, mouth, teeth, throat, and tongue, such as ulcers, gum issues, bad breath, breathing issues, and numerous teeth problems. Moreover, you may also experience issues such as gossiping, dominating conversations, struggling with voicing your concerns honestly and may often speak without thinking. All these problems keep you from building happy, genuine, and meaningful relationships.

Also, you may have trouble admitting your feelings to yourself. You may deny your concerns, refute your ideas, and never believe in yourself when the throat chakra has been blocked. But when it's aligned, you listen to others compassionately, understand things from different perspectives, think before speaking, and express yourself clearly, confidently, and very comfortably.

Using the 741 Hz frequency regularly in your life helps you cleanse the throat chakra and build a positive relationship with yourself and others. Let us take a look at how you can achieve this goal.

- Find a relaxing beat on the 741 Hz frequency like this one (https://youtu.be/q3YRTZGKx8Q) and listen to it daily for at least 5 minutes. Gradually, increase the duration to listen to it for extended lengths, such as 20 to 30 minutes.
- Whenever possible, play this tune in the background, so you listen to it throughout the day, and slowly heal your throat chakra-related issues with this practice.
- Also, whenever possible, gently close your eyes and locate the spot of the throat chakra. Imagine a soft and comforting blue-colored ball of light entering your throat. With every breath you take, picture the blue light growing more extensive and more powerful.

Imagine it has grown, and it has spread to every part of your body and is radiating outside. With that, envision all the energy obstructions exiting your body, leaving you reassured, poised, and happy.

- Think of whatever things you wish to talk about with confidence and clarity, and imagine yourself voicing those concerns very easily. Moreover, slowly encourage yourself to say whatever is on your mind in social situations, so you practice what you believe in. Openly speaking comes with courage and practice, so you need to take that action step to make it possible.

Make sure that these practices become constants in your life to reap their actual benefits. Let us now move to the sixth frequency from the solfeggio sequence in the next chapter.

Chapter 10: LA- 852 Hz- Awakens Your Intuition

The sixth solfeggio frequency is that of LA that operates on a frequency of 852 Hz. 852 is divisible by 6, so this frequency runs on the power of the number 6. Let us find out more about it in this chapter.

LA Helps Stimulate Your Intuitive Capabilities

As you climb up the scale of the lowest to highest solfeggio frequencies, you would have noticed how you are going all the way up the higher planes of your consciousness, finally tapping into your intuition to awaken the spiritual connection with yourself. The note 'LA' helps you do this trick nicely.

LA is the sixth and the last of the fundamental solfeggio frequencies. There are three more of these, which were discovered later on.

The frequency of 852 Hz has the magnificent power to connect you directly with the universe, so you become a part of it and can sense its mighty force bubbling inside of you. Plus, it gives you a sneak peek into the spiritual world around you, so you feel stimulated to tap into your own higher self and build an unwavering association with it for good.

Often in life, we feel as if there is more to ourselves, but somehow we are unable to explore that dimension to our personality. We sense a constant sense of void in our lives, but we fail to understand its roots. We feel as if our life lacks a clear sense of direction, but once again, we cannot pinpoint the reason behind the issue. We keep hoping to make the most of our time and energy every day but come to nothing meaningful. We lack the drive, passion, and enthusiasm to do something more significant in life, and that feeling does not sit well with us.

These concerns are rooted in a lack of spiritual connection with ourselves. Spirituality is often associated with faith, but basically, its essence lies in feeling in tune with your body, mind, and spirit to the extent that all of them feel united. It is only when your heart, body, and soul are aligned that you start to explore your sense of purpose in life. You realize you aren't just here to breathe, eat, sleep and do all of this in repeat, but there is a lot more to your existence, so you start to dig into the mystery.

The more you delve into it, the more puzzle pieces you find out, and then you start connecting the dots to find the hidden nexus amongst everything. It takes you time to conclude, but eventually, you figure everything out and realize your inner calling. This realization is what your awakening is about. You understand your purpose and embark on different journeys, one after another, to steer your life in a meaningful direction.

During this process, you unlock your intuitive voice and use it for guidance. You realize how all the information, knowledge, and guidance for living better has been lying inside you all these years. You just needed to tap into the reservoir to set the wisdom free. You start paying better heed to your gut feeling, allowing it to direct you towards the right paths in life. Soon enough, your life starts to brim with meaning, empowerment, and value, and everything changes for the better.

The 852 Hz frequency brings about this transformation in you by clearing up the toxic energies in your mind, body, and spirit and aligning your third eye chakra.

LA and the Third Eye Chakra

The third eye chakra is the sixth of the seven major ones. Known as *Ajna* in Sanskrit, it is located right in the middle of your eyes, which is why it is often referred to as the 'brow' chakra.

It is associated with the color 'indigo' and is in charge of your imaginative and intuitive capabilities. As it is positioned right in the center of your eyebrows on your forehead, it also controls your forehead, eyes, face, and neck. Energy obstructions in the Ajna chakra often manifest themselves in the form of painful headaches, eye irritations, poor eyesight, and conditions related to your face, as well as hearing issues.

Moreover, if the third eye chakra is closed or blocked, you find it challenging to tune into your gut feeling and seek any advice from it. Every time you are faced with a decision, you feel clueless and confused from within. You either get myriads of mixed answers or hear nothing at all. You feel chaotic and just don't know what to do, which keeps you from making an informed decision. You are likely to experience problems with exploring ideas imaginatively. You fail to analyze situations from different angles and take different things into perspective to develop innovative approaches to solve many of your problems in life.

When your brow chakra is open and vibrating optimally, you think creatively and find it easier to re-center yourself to take different perspectives into account. You also feel in tune with your spiritual self and easily seek guidance from your intuitive voice to make worthwhile life choices.

The chakra has a frequency of 852 Hz, so the LA note works best in cleansing it. Let us take a look at how you can bring about this cleansing.

How to Use the 852 Hz Frequency to Stimulate Your Intuition

It is best to work with the 852 Hz frequency once you have experimented with the previous ones. The five frequencies discussed earlier lay down the foundation for your body, mind, and spirit to work in harmony with each other and become more receptive to a higher frequency.

If you start with the 852 Hz frequency right away, you may feel some inner resistance to accept it, and that usually happens due to energy blockages in any of the lower five chakras. Once you have at least opened your first five chakras, it is time to move on to the sixth one. Here is what you need to do:

- Begin by spending a few minutes daily listening to a tune created by the 852 Hz frequency. Try this one, (https://youtu.be/aJ2gDWirnYU) and you are pretty likely to feel mesmerized by it.

- When listening to the beat, keep an open mind and accept its rhythm as it is without jumping to any judgments or labels. Judging things is the second nature of many of us. While it seems like something meaningless and harmless, this habit that we have formed over the years is detrimental to our wellbeing. When we are too quick to judge anything or put the label of 'bad' on it, we keep ourselves from exploring the idea. It may be possible that the concept or thing may be what your soul seeks, but we keep ourselves from experimenting with it because we have already declared it to be useless. Do not allow this habit to restrain you from exploring and enjoying the glory of the 852 Hz frequency. So whatever judgments may pop in your head, gently discard them and realign your attention on the beat. Once you do that, you find yourself losing to the frequency's beat and focus on it well.

- Close your eyes, locate the spot of your Ajna chakra, and imagine an indigo-colored, powerful light entering it and gradually intensifying with every breath you take. Picture it dispersing all over your head, neck, face, and the rest of your body, helping it relax and awaken in the process. Practice it for 5 to 10 minutes at least two to three times every week.

Incorporate these practices in your daily life to allow the solfeggio frequencies to change your destiny. This brings our discussion on the ancient and elementary solfeggio frequencies to a close. You may be wondering how come I haven't discussed the seventh chakra while I categorically mentioned that 7 of 114 chakras are incredibly crucial throughout the book. I said earlier how Dr. Leonard Horowitz discovered three more frequencies. Of those three, the highest one corresponds to the seventh chakra and is accompanied by two low-range frequencies. Let us explore them in the following chapter.

Chapter 11: 963 Hz Unlocks Your Divine Consciousness

The 963 Hz frequency is the highest frequency tune of the nine solfeggio frequencies, and for this reason, it is often referred to as the most powerful of the lot. Let us learn more about its transforming powers here.

The Frequency of Divine Awareness

This frequency builds up on the previous one. While the 852 Hz frequency opens your intuition, the 963 Hz helps it advance on many levels. It hones on your consciousness, scales it up, and makes you reach the highest plane of self-awareness, spirituality as well as a consciousness of the world around you.

No matter what faith you believe in, or even if you don't advocate for one, you probably do believe that this universe possesses unimaginable power that is all-reaching and affects every being in it. The truth is, we can become one with that oneness that permeates each and everything. This happens when we reach the highest level of our consciousness and unleash its full potential. This is where the 963 Hz frequency serves its purpose. It awakens the highest of the seven prominent chakras, the crown chakra, and turns you into your most potent and magnificent self ever.

The Crown Chakra and 963 Hz Solfeggio Frequency

The crown chakra, known as *Sahasrara* in Sanskrit, lies at the crown of your head- right at the top. It vibrates at the frequency of 963 Hz frequency, which is divisible by 9; hence, it encapsulates this number's essence. It is associated with the 'violet' color and is known to bring forth a splendid revolution in your existence and life.

Your crown chakra is connected to your pineal gland that forms your central nervous system and plays a vital role in determining your life's purpose. It is connected to all the other chakras and so directly affects them and all the organs they govern. Plus, it directly impacts your brain and nervous system, which means energy congestions here lead to neurological and immune system disorders.

This is the chakra of enlightenment which means once you open and align it, it helps you truly understand and actualize your inner calling, so you feel empowered from every inch of your body. Gradually, you become telepathic, build psychic vision, feel intuitive all the time, and discover your intimate bond with the divine force in the universe.

When the crown chakra is closed and obstructed, you are likely to become obstinate, skeptical of different situations in life, and act narrow-mindedly in every experience you encounter. You are resistant to new ideas, hesitate to experiment in life and prefer staying stuck in your cocoon of low self-esteem.

When your crown chakra is open and actively vibrating,

you realize how your life is full of meaning. You start to observe and study yourself, your thoughts, different situations, and ideas in life closely and objectively to make more sense of them. That is when you make novel discoveries in life and find true meaning in it.

Moreover, when your crown chakra functions optimally, so do the rest of the six ones, consequently restoring harmony and balance in your body. Since changes and problems are a part of life, they may still affect you, but with an active crown chakra, you find it easy to counteract those troubles and find inner peace.

Let us now show you how you can achieve this goal with the 963 Hz frequency.

How to Best use the 963 Hz Frequency

Before starting with the following measures, set an intention with yourself to unlock your highest mental and intuitive faculties to live a meaningful life. With this intention, you practice the following with dedication and achieve desirable results:

- Set a time of the day when you are free and can devotedly listen to a beat on the 963 Hz frequency. Try this (https://youtu.be/8_yCzcU4fwo) one as it has a very magical appeal to it. Remember to do so in a relaxed pose and allow your ears and mind to focus on the beat to absorb your subconscious better and fully.
- As you listen to it, visualize yourself feeling completely light, energized, and free from all sorts of worries in the world. Imagine that you have achieved

enlightenment and are now aware of every secret about yourself those of the universe. You are floating high above in the universe, observing everything clearly from the highest plane there exists. Add colors, expressions, feelings, and sounds to this visualization, and you will feel more engrossed in it.

- While listening to the 936 Hz beats, or right after, think of any monumental aspect of your life you are trying to improve. Tune into your intuition, and pay attention to the feelings and ideas you get. For instance, if you often think about your purpose in life, ask yourself what it truly is, and write down whatever answers you hear from inside you. Contemplate those ideas as much as possible to make sense of them. The more you deeply reflect on your thoughts, the better you explore them, and the more you hone your intuitive capabilities.

For better results, document your journey with solfeggio frequencies in your journal. Write down about the practices you try, your feelings before and after every exercise, and how consistently you observe them. You can even record yourself speaking about these experiences if documenting long written accounts is difficult for you. Ensure to go through these audio or written entries every week to track your performance.

So far, we have discussed 7 of the nine solfeggio frequencies. Let us delve into the remaining two in the following chapter.

Chapter 12: Frequencies 174 and 285 Hz

The frequencies 174 Hz and 285 Hz were identified by Dr. Leonard Horowitz and are two low tone frequencies that yield potent results on your body, mind, and spirit.

Solfeggio Frequency of 174 Hz

This is the lowest of the solfeggio beats, and it affects our mind and spirit on the lowest plane and our physical energy and body. It is often referred to as a natural anesthetic that helps relieve all sorts of pains from your body. It improves your organs' functioning by nurturing them and instilling a sense of comfort and security in them.

Naturally, when your organs feel cared for, they function effectively and efficiently, improving your overall physical wellbeing. Since physical wellbeing affects your emotional and psychological wellbeing, you start to feel happier and peaceful as your physical health improves.

Action Step:

Start listening to beats on a 174 Hz frequency such as this one. (https://youtu.be/RJwZE7Peocc) It has a very earthy, reassuring feel to it that is soothing to your ears and mind. Allow yourself to become immersed in its rhythm, and imagine yourself becoming free of every pain, discomfort, and ailment.

Solfeggio Frequency of 285 Hz

The second low frequency of the solfeggio clan vibrates at 285 Hz. It penetrates further in your body compared to the 174 Hz beat and promotes healing in your skin, tissues, muscles, and any burns, lacerations, and injuries you have incurred in life.

This beat also improves your physical wellbeing and emotional health by rejuvenating your energy levels, spirit, mind, and body. Basically, the frequencies 174 and 285 are healing beats for the human body. As the other beats take care of our soul, mind, and DNA, these two beats mainly focus on your physical body to ensure you attain holistic health and wellbeing.

Action Step:

Listen to music and rhythms operational on the 285 Hz frequency such as this one here. (https://youtu.be/e-0Ic2hpgEQ) Ensure you are settled in a calm environment as you keenly listen to the music and meditate on it peacefully. Imagine yourself in a serene atmosphere, cleansed of all kinds of physical conditions and problems, feeling happy and prosperous. Work on this practice for 10 minutes daily, and wear more earthy tones to promote healing throughout your body.

Chapter 13: Solfeggio Frequencies and the Ancient Chinese Lushu in I-Ching

The 'I Ching,' also known as the 'Yi Jing' in Chinese, is an ancient divination text in Chinese and is revered amongst the most ancient Chinese classics. Translated as the *'Classic of Changes'* or *'Book of Changes,'* this book was originally incepted as a divination manual during the Western Zhou period and was eventually turned into a cosmological text accompanied by different philosophical commentaries that are referred to as the *'Ten Wings.'*

The I Ching has served as the subject of many scholarly commentaries. It has also served as the fundamental basis for practicing and learning divination all over the Far East. Soon after, it gained its way into the Western world and attained massive popularity. It is also believed that I Ching and the solfeggio frequencies share quite a strong association. Let us explore that in this chapter.

Chinese Lushu in I Ching and Solfeggio Frequencies

Cleromancy is a kind of divination used in I Ching that makes use of random numbers. Six numbers are taken between the numbers 6 and 9 and used to create a hexagram.

When the hexagrams are moved in a particular order, they form the '*King Wen sequence.*' The readings have different interpretations that have been used for centuries by people believing in Buddhism, Taoism, and Confucianism to make different life decisions. These hexagrams have attained huge cosmological importance over time and have also been linked to having connections with the solfeggio frequencies.

The squares in the Lo Shu (Lushu) grid are also known as magic squares. Back in the days when they were discovered, their meaning was derived from combining the cosmological belief system with routine life. The Kabbalists used magic squares as talismans or charms to protect themselves from evil spirits and draw good fortune towards themselves.

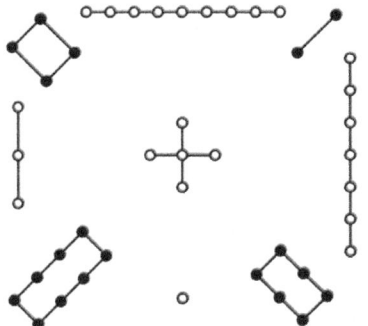

The Christians and Gnostics too relied on magic squares in their everyday life and used them on the covers of their holy manuscripts. As for the Shang Chinese people, the Lo Shu was incorporated in the planning of their cities as well as designing temples. The cosmological and numerological aspects of the Lo Shu were also used in the Chinese language to create political assertiveness and command over the people.

These squares have gained massive popularity in the Western World after Agrippa's De Occulta Philosophia was published in 1533. This is because the manuscript described how to use those squares in the best possible manner in Alchemy and Magic. It may not have been practical, but it was definitely a prevalent usage at that time.

Using the numerology vibration of each solfeggio frequencies, we discovered their connections with the Lo Shu as described below.

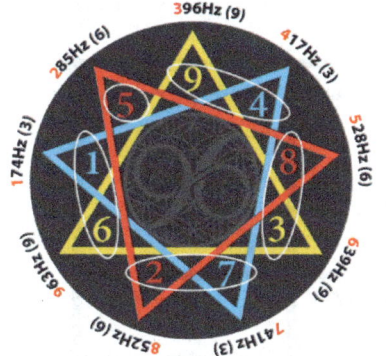 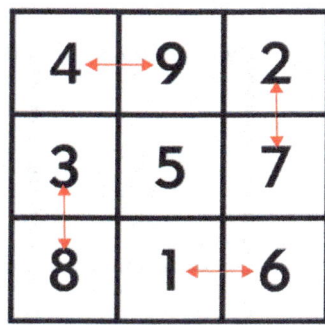

(for calculation please refer to Numerology Vibrations-Calculation Chart, e.g.; 417 = 4)

In the above circular chart you can see -

yellow triangle is (396 Hz – 639 Hz – 963 Hz)

Red triangle is (285 Hz – 528 Hz – 852 Hz)

Blue triangle is (174 Hz – 417 Hz – 741 Hz)

They are in line with the Lo Shu numbers:

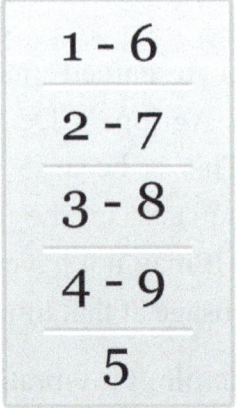

So we can see the Yin and Yang of the solfeggio frequencies (1, 3, 5, 7, 9 is Yang and 2, 4, 6, 8 is Yin)

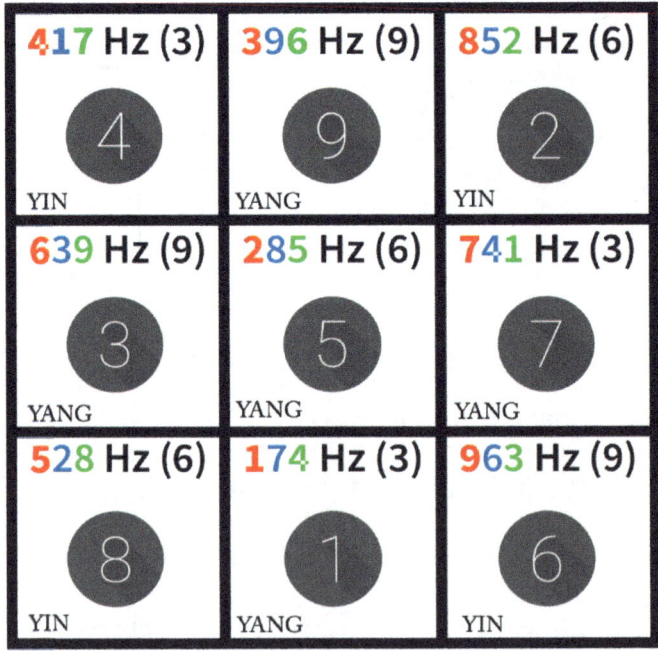

With the above chart we can apply the correct solfeggio frequencies of yin and yang to anyone base on their birth dates calculations

Below are 3 x 3 Square with solfeggio frequencies 3 numbers, using loshu magic square sequence they all amazingly added up to 6

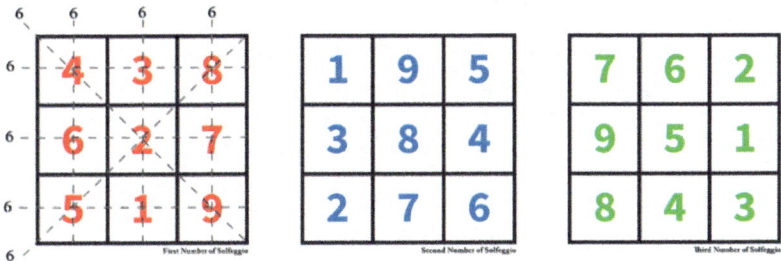

Box one is the first number of the solfeggio

Box two the second number of the solfeggio

Box three is the third number of the solfeggio

Magic Square and Musical Tones

Peter Maxwell Davies and John Cage have generated some brilliant musical materials like rhythm and pitch using the magic squares.

John Milton Cage, a composer of American origin, was indeed an influential and inspiring composer from the twentieth century. 'Music of Changes' is a striking solo piano piece he has created.

Peter Maxwell Davies, another talented composer but of English origin, has made use of magic squares in many of the tunes that he has composed. If you are a classical music enthusiast, you are likely to be aware of 'Ave Maris.' That composition was made in 1975, and was structured on the foundation of the 9 x 9 magic square of 'Moon.' Another of his compositions, 'Stella', too follows the same magic square. 'A Mirror of Whitening Light' is also his creation that he launched in 1977, and is created using the 8 x 8 'Mercury' magic square. These are not his only compositions that are created with the help of the magic squares. Joining this list are 'Resurrection', launched in 1987, 'The Lighthouse', created in 1979, and 'Strathclyde Concerto No.3 for Horn and Trumpet' in 1989 along with many other amazing symphonies.

Davies describes the magic squares in a musical symphony as a founding principle that one needs to learn, understand and perceive inwardly as something with multiple dimensions. It is not really a mere group of numbers. It goes far beyond that. When you project a magic square onto a page, it is just a combination of numbers. It is only when it takes the form of a musical composition that one gets to experience and relish its enormous power. That's when you tune into an inspiring, transformational and powerful dynamic of stunning musical images that open your mind and soul, and broaden your horizon.

I believe this does describe the power of magic squares rather beautifully and clarifies any ambiguities that you may have had pertaining to their force. They are not really a concoction of numbers. They are power. They are magic. And they are transformational for sure. It is only when we start listening to the solfeggio frequencies that we start to harness the power of the magic squares for real.

Conclusion

———————❦———————

There is magic inside of you and the universe. The sooner you acknowledge and channelize it, the easier it will be for you to thrive in this world. I have provided you just the proper knowledge you need to make this happen in the form of solfeggio frequencies.

Now, the reins are in your hands.

You can bring forth unbelievable transformation in life.

You can be the extraordinary being you are meant to be.

You can harness the power of the divine force and use it to benefit every being in this universe.

Yes, it is all possible, and the universe is waiting for you to tap into its power. Get started with exercising the guidelines in this book and ignite the fire in you.

Links

1. https://www.westcoastyogaperth.com/2020/06/30/solfeggio-frequencies-and-the-chakras/

2. https://www.binauralbeatsfreak.com/sound-therapy/solfeggio-frequencies-chakra-system

3. https://www.mindvibrations.com/ancient-solfeggio-scale/

4. https://medium.com/illumination/how-to-heal-your-mind-and-body-with-powerful-sounds-c8ee64a1dbd

5. https://ptolemy.berkeley.edu/eecs20/week8/scale.html

6. https://nexidy.com/articles/84-the-magnificence-of-3-6-and-9

7. https://www.buggedspace.com/tesla-3-6-9-theory-and-why-he-called-it-key-to-universe/

8. https://www.relaxmelodies.com/blog/science-behind-solfeggio-frequencies/

9. https://www.gaia.com/article/healing-frequencies-of-the-ancient-solfeggio-scale

10. https://www.mindvibrations.com/ancient-solfeggio-scale/

11. https://www.relaxmelodies.com/blog/science-behind-solfeggio-frequencies/

12. https://www.binauralbeatsfreak.com/sound-therapy/solfeggio-frequencies-guide

13. https://www.gaia.com/article/healing-frequencies-of-the-ancient-solfeggio-scale

Made in the USA
Coppell, TX
20 April 2023

15867422R00056